TERRIBLE THINGS

happened to me

**A TRUE STORY OF VIOLENCE
AND VICTORY**

TOM SCALES

Cover design and illustration by Mark Sandlin
Production design by Felicia Kahn

Library of Congress Cataloging-in-Publication Data
1 – Biography; 2 – American Families; 3 – Incest; 4 - Child Sexual Abuse
Terrible Things Happened to Me
Thomas A. Scales, Marietta, Georgia, USA

ISBN.0-000-0000-0

This book is dedicated to the millions of adult survivors of child sexual abuse.

I hope that in some way, it touches your heart and helps you to begin the process of sincere and real healing.

Proceeds from this book will go to VOICE Today, Inc. to support their passionate efforts to break the silence and the cycle of child sexual abuse.

ACKNOWLEDGMENTS

The existence of this book is truly a miracle and I thank God for opening my heart and guiding my pen to tell my story.

He used a number of important people to encourage, help and prod me. First on that list is my wife, Liza, whose patience and wisdom through the darkest years, and support during the writing, were invaluable to both the healing and the writing.

Knowing only pieces of the story, my children, Pat and Sarah, have encouraged me to write. Their love and support was critical to the transformation of my life.

Angela Williams, her book, and VOICE Today, Inc. gave me a purpose in life and constant encouragement to use my experiences and my story to reach and support other survivors. She modeled the self-sacrifice that comes with such a deep and personal exposition and her example gave me the courage to complete the book.

To my many friends at VOICE, and those I have met through VOICE, I thank you for the wisdom, love, and friendship that you share with me every day.

In some way the imprint of these wonderful people appears on each page.

CONTENTS

INTRODUCTION

You enter a room and meet a new person or chat with a friend. You share a coffee and exchange pleasantries, but you rarely get to "know" the person in front of you. Every individual comes with a story that may show joy, excitement and accomplishment. On the other hand, it may be filled with fear, rage, heartache, and shame. These stories are frequently not on the surface because truly knowing a person requires a bridge of trust. Telling that story can be a giant step of faith and listening can be a challenging exercise in compassion and love. I invite you to walk with me for a while and get to really know the man in my story. Feel the confusion and sense the fear of violence and abuse that visited me on a regular basis. Understand my dread of the possibility that someone would discover my horrible secret, while at the same time I prayed for my rescue. Listen as the adults around me talk about honesty, commitment, trust, and truth, and then watch the contradicting depravity of their actions. Look with me for someone to tell, and then feel my anxiety and frustration as individuals, whom I thought would be a safe haven, become predators.

What would you do? Where would you turn? As an innocent child you ask yourself over and over again: What words do I use to describe what is happening? Will they believe me? Will they call me a liar? Will they be repulsed by what I say or what I have done? See how I tried to cope with the sense of abandonment conveyed by those around me. How would you cope? As a survivor, you may relate in a deep and personal way to my experiences.

This is my story and my life that I offer. If you are not a survivor, I encourage you to learn from my story so that you have a greater understanding and are better prepared when you have the opportunity to support and encourage the healing of another. If you are a survivor, I invite you on this journey of understanding and healing with me. You may have seen horrific times as I have. You may have suffered the physical abuse, humiliation, shame, guilt and self-loathing as I have. Like me, you may have had no place to go for safety and protection. After decades of suffering, I have found a new life of peace, happiness, joy, self-respect, and self-love. I have shed the guilt, shame, and other self-destructive attitudes that haunted my life. Through my story, I encourage you to consider these as new possibilities for your life. I believe that one man's life can be another man's lesson. I hope and pray that there is a worthwhile lesson here for you.

What terror and violence has visited your life? Has it been child sexual abuse, as in my case, or has it been something else? It is my hope and prayer that those who read this book will see my transitions from victim to survivor, and then from survivor to victor over the trauma of child sexual abuse as a distinct possibility for their lives. Victory and healing are available to all, regardless of how the damage was inflicted, regardless of age, sex, race, economic status, or any other factor you wish to consider. Shedding guilt, fear, shame, and all the self-destructive behaviors used to cope is possible for all, regardless of how many predators or how many times you were abused.

For many years my life was XXX-rated. As a survivor, you understand the significance of that. If you are not a survivor, it may be difficult for you to grasp how it feels to live a life that is so evil and so disgusting that you can't talk about it in public. In this book, I talk about it. I want my story to help free survivors to realize that these events do not have to dominate, control, or define your life and your future. There can be peace, joy, and self-respect. But healing is work and is not for the faint-hearted. It is not something someone else can do for you, and there is no amount of money that can buy the final product.

WHY EVEN PICK UP THIS PEN?

My motive for writing this book is not to draw attention to me as an individual or to generate sympathy or tears about the experiences of my youth. It is not intended to be offensive or overly graphic. Although it may be difficult to read in certain parts, I have tried to avoid many of the more gruesome details. At the same time, society has carefully wrapped the violent and destructive acts associated with child sexual abuse in two "comfortable" words – abuse and molestation. Maybe this allows our culture to cope with events without being overwhelmed by the horrific evil that actually occurs. Today these words mute the real trauma – the torture, violation, and manipulation of a child's life, and understate dramatically the grisly and gruesome nature of the violation.

Last, my book is definitely not meant to provide any titillating excitement about my path to "manhood." What really happened was the brutal theft of the beauty and joy of the relationship with my wife.

I have not specifically identified the many predators who assaulted me. They don't deserve such recognition. Their names are irrelevant and they are unimportant to my overall purpose for the book. My hope and prayer is that this book will be a guide for those traveling a similar path to mine in helping them find healing and restoration.

There will also be many who will get through at least a few pages and then think, "How could he have possibly talk out loud about the things done to him, or worse, done by him as part of the abuse?" For you who have trouble reading my story because it is so horrible or disgusting, I can only say that it is much easier to read it than it was and is to live it. Just ask any survivor of child sexual abuse who will also tell you there is nothing unusual or exceptionally awful about my sufferings.

This book is written for the millions of silent survivors of child sexual abuse in the United States of America and around the world – individuals who have suffered unspeakable violence at the hands of family, friends, and strangers and in most cases have never spoken about it. It is a terrible secret that many victims spend enormous amounts of energy to hide, using countless defense mechanisms in order to function – even survive – every day. The initial sections of this book are intended to share sufficient details of my abuse so that other survivors can connect with and relate to my experiences. I want you to know that I truly understand your pain and suffering; I understand much of the violence you have endured.

Today, I carry no guilt or shame for my abuse. That belongs only to the predators who damaged my body, mind, and heart, but who never took my soul. My salvation through Jesus Christ and the trustworthy people God has placed around me have helped me restore my life by redirecting my thoughts and softening my heart, thereby allowing me to trust again. Today I feel great about myself and the mission I have in life. I am blessed to have true, honest, and honorable friendships and a family who has stood by me and loved me through the darkest of times. I want every survivor to feel as I do today, and I want every child to be protected from the path I had to travel to get there. This is my purpose for this book.

2

GROWING UP BLIND

I was born and raised in Charleston, West Virginia, the fourth of five boys. My mother was a medical technologist at a local chemical company and for many years my father was a mortician. He later sold the mortuary and bought a hardware store where I worked many hours after school and on weekends. Our family was a good Catholic bunch. My parents, at my mother's insistence, had us in Sacred Heart Church at every possible opportunity. I attended Sacred Heart Elementary School and went on to graduate from Charleston Catholic High School. Mostly, Franciscan nuns taught my classes and they seemed to have an instant communication channel to my parents. The concept of doing what I was told was drilled into me daily. Over and over I heard that adults know best and children should listen, obey, and not be heard. This mantra would play a pivotal role in my future.

While I grew up in a house with 4 siblings, I have little, if any, memory of interacting with them or them interacting with my parents. In some ways when I look back at my childhood, it almost seems like I was an only child and no one else was there. I do remember dividing everything 5 ways, especially food, but I remember very few meals together. I remember doing chores. My job was to clean the bathroom, but I couldn't tell you any jobs my brothers had. I remember cutting the grass, but don't remember anyone else doing it. This doesn't mean that they didn't have jobs or weren't there. I can't imagine they got any different or better treatment than I did. What it means is that all those memories have been blanked out for some reason.

My earliest childhood memory is of my father accusing me of stealing a nickel from my mother's dresser. I told him I didn't take it and didn't have it, but his mind was made up. It didn't seem to impact him that I could not reach the shelf from where I supposedly took the coin. He punished me by making me put all my belongings into a box and then he threw me out of the house. I can hear his harsh voice as he handed me the box, told me to put my things in it, and then said, "We don't want a boy who would steal in our house."

The meanness in his voice was frightening. He also told me not to go to my grandparents, who live two blocks away. Then he opened the back door, showed me out, and then closed it quickly behind me. I sat on the back steps and cried; I was 5-years-old and had never felt so alone. While my mother subsequently let me back in, she did so without so much as a hug or a gentle word to assure me that I was loved or welcome. Her terse guidance was "Don't make your father mad." From that moment, I believed that I was only one misstep from being discarded by my family. This belief stuck with me for decades. From that moment on, I lived in constant fear of my father and knew I was no different from the kitchen trash or an empty box or bag. I was disposable.

There are many examples of my father's discipline. I remember arguing once with one of my brothers, so he demonstrated his conflict resolution skills. He made us put on boxing gloves and fight each other. When we didn't want to fight, he insisted.

On another occasion, I was fighting with another brother outside. He took a pitchfork, put it up to my chest and told me to pick on someone my own size. Looking back, I don't believe it was his actions that were so mean spirited and intimidating, but his words and his tone. They conveyed a ruthlessness and meanness that was scary. He often left me feeling worthless and hated.

Life lesson #1 was to stay out of sight, keep my mouth shut, and do nothing that could be deemed bad or wrong because the consequences could be catastrophic. In the final analysis, abiding by this lesson was to have its own catastrophic consequences of a very different nature.

When my mother would get frustrated with having five boys in the house, or we did not do what we were told, she would simply get dressed up and tell us that she was leaving and never coming back. If we did exactly as we were told, she would reconsider. I remember times when I begged through my tears for her not to leave. If my father's actions delivered a message that my place in the family was always at risk, my mother confirmed it with certainty by her apparent willingness to walk away and not come back. Life lesson #2 was that our value was totally dependent on performance.

The sense of rejection and abandonment I felt was profound and surfaced frequently as fear and insecurity through most of my adult life. I thought this was normal behavior and it never occurred to me that my friends did not live in the same kind of environment. I had no idea how to love, much less love unconditionally, because I didn't feel loved. I didn't' know how it felt to receive love and, as a result, I raised barriers anytime anyone tried to get close. I instinctively built relationships based on people meeting performance expectations I had.

As a child of the 40's and 50's, I was raised to never question authority and to accept that adults always knew best. Performance and obedience were all that counted. I worked many hours in my father's hardware store to please him and earn his love. I sold paint, small appliances and grass seed, cut and threaded pipe, stocked shelves, and took inventory. It was a thrilling moment one Saturday when my father paid me for working ten hours when the store had its best sales day ever. He dropped the coin into my hand, and when I looked down, I saw it was a shiny Ben Franklin fifty-cent piece. I hoped at that moment that I had found a way to my father's heart. Events like this gave me the encouragement to work harder for my father's attention and love. There were even times when he left me alone to tend the store and I interpreted this as a giant step in meeting his expectations and earning his trust.

In spite of all the hours I put into the hardware store, he became angry on the one occasion I didn't want to help do inventory. My punishment was to sit on a wooden bench at home for the eight hours he was at the store. There was no excuse my mother would accept for me to leave that bench.

My father was a big, imposing, and aloof figure. I don't ever remember sitting on his lap, getting a hug or hearing a kind word. My greatest fear was facing his anger. Getting spanked was not a trivial exercise in our house. He did it like he really meant it and you remembered how hard he hit you. How often this actually occurred I don't know, but it left an indelible impression. His goal seemed to be focused on inflicting as much fear as possible so there would never be at time when I wouldn't do exactly what I was told. It is difficult to figure out where his sense of discipline and fairness came from. He was an only child and his mother was a very kind and gentle soul. In contrast, his father and grandfather were distant, hard and rigid men. Years later, my mother told my wife that she just couldn't understand how such a sweet woman as my grandmother could have married such a tyrant and slave master as my grandfather. She also told about the anniversary gift he presented to my grandmother – it was a check for $100 and on the memo line it said "For 50 years of faithful service." None of us were surprised when my dear, loving grandmother descended into senility after the death of her husband. We all believed it was a release from years of stress, living with a man who treated her like a slave. The difference between the two of them was never more obvious than when we cut their grass. You could spend hours cutting the grass, trimming the yard with hand clippers, raking up the crabapples and then sweeping and finishing the job. He would come out, and without a word, generously give us 25-50 cents. She in turn would come quietly behind and slip us $5 and a big smile of thanks.

I have very few memories of childhood – no happy Christmases, no trips to the zoo, no family picnics, and no fun vacations. Those events may have occurred, but if they did, the memories are lost in the terrifying turmoil of my youth. Things would get a lot worse before they got better.

3

THE TERROR TAKES MANY FORMS

It all began one night when I awoke with someone on top of me. My underpants were down and I was being sodomized. The experience was horrifically painful and scary. Almost immediately afterward, the nightmares began and I suffered through them on most nights, even into adulthood. While I only remember it happening one time, the impact stayed with me for decades. When I slept I would be terrorized by shadowy images, and excruciating pain; I recognized that the failure of my mother or father to come to my rescue not only confirmed that I was disposable, but also it meant that I could be used and abused as anyone saw fit. That nocturnal invasion exacerbated my fears and I knew home was not a safe place for me. So, at the earliest age possible, I tried to find ways out of the house and into safer environments. My efforts, however, turned into one bad decision after another.

What safer place could there be than church? It made perfect sense to follow in a family tradition of sorts and become an altar boy. In the beginning, it served its purpose well and I enjoyed serving. I felt special to be chosen frequently to participate in many services including daily and Sunday masses, weddings, and funerals. Then one day the priest invited me back to the living area adjacent to the church. He was a warm and friendly man and everyone always felt relaxed and comfortable around him. My mother even told me from time-to-time that she hoped I would become a priest just like him. It never occurred to me that he was anything but God's spokesperson in our parish.

With my blind and childish trust, I followed him, even excited that I would be chosen for such special treatment. He led me into a room with a bed and sat down. His voice was encouraging, uplifting, and calming, and I was thrilled and excited that for once, someone seemed to actually like having me around. I finally had a safe place where someone would protect me.

He asked me to kneel in front of him and close my eyes so he could pray especially just for me. I wondered if God was finally going to shine His light of blessing on me. As he prayed, he spoke about what a wonderful child I was and how committed I was to be doing all that God asked of me. I couldn't believe this was me we were talking about. I had never heard such praise and appreciation before. He moved his hand to the back of my neck, massaging it at first, and then firmly gripping it as he softly told me to open my eyes. It was then I realized that he had pulled back his clothing and was naked underneath. He was also aroused. He told me that I needed to service him so that he could properly serve God and that this was a very important part of God's work and my contribution to it.

My mind was quickly spinning and I had no understanding of what was happening or how to react. As I instinctively started to pull back, his grip became stronger. I only felt a powerful sense of fear, confusion, and revulsion. He forced me to hold and massage his erection and then he put it in my mouth. My terror was overwhelming. The tears flowed uncontrollably. When he was finished with me, he simply said that he would excommunicate me and embarrass my parents if I ever told a soul what had happened. Could there be any more terrible event in my life than being "excommunicated?" This event was repeated many times in one form or another, including him performing oral sex and sodomizing me. The "good Father" was revered and respected by my parents and continued to be a frequent dinner guest in our home. He sometimes took that opportunity to "pray" with me at bedtime – usually with his hands under my covers. Many times, my parents were only steps away but they never noticed or interrupted what the priest was doing. But I questioned what God was doing and why this was happening to me, just a vulnerable young boy.

When I tried to avoid the priest, he went into the kitchen on one visit and talked quietly with my mother. He apparently told her I was starting to "act up" at church and he was worried that I was picking up some bad habits. He told her I might have to stop my role as an altar boy if my behavior didn't improve: "God doesn't want bad boys around."

My Mother wasted no time cornering me and saying with a crystal clear voice that I should do "exactly what Father instructed me to do" or she would tell my father and I would have to answer to him. The fear of my father was more powerful than the sexual violation of my body and betrayal of trust by a priest.

With my compliance safely assured, Father frequently took me to that same room in the rectory. On one occasion when we got there, he told me to remove my clothes and he removed his. Lying on the bed together, he told me to massage his erection and I did it. He then told me to put his penis in my mouth, but I hesitated and just laid there. He gently reached down and fondled my genitals for a few seconds and then said that it was important that I always do as he asked and that I show him that I enjoy being with him and bringing him pleasure.

He then said, "This is going to hurt, but I want you to come to me with enthusiasm and enjoy me as much as I enjoy you. Once you show this to me, I will stop what I am about to do." He then took my penis between his thumb and forefinger and began to squeeze – harder and harder.

As I started to cry and scream, he simply said, "You can make the pain stop by sucking on me as hard as you can. I thought he was going to pinch off my penis. I had never felt such pain. As I did everything I could for him, he finally let go. And when he was done, he said, "Thank you Tom. That felt really wonderful." There seemed to be certain exhilaration in his voice, a sense of power and dominance as he controlled me with brutal force.

As he started to stand up, the door opened, and I instantly felt a moment of relief and hoped my rescue was there, but I was wrong. In stepped a second priest and he closed the door. The first priest looked at him and said, "Tom has something wonderful to show you, but you have to take your pants off first."

He did just that and sat on the bed next to me, and with a kind voice asked me to show him what I had learned. I just lay there with his erection staring me in the face, feeling sick, filthy, and disgusting and wanting to die. When I didn't move, he knew what to do and reached over and caressed my penis and then slowly began to squeeze. When the pain became more than I could handle, I serviced him. All the while the two of them talked about how terrific it felt for me to do this for them and how we will all have more wonderful times in the future. When I left them that day, I walked out the door to the parking lot, threw up, went to the grade school and rinsed my mouth with water and walked home.

From that time on, the two of them shared me, sometimes one-on-one and sometimes both of them on me. The times when it was the two of them with me were particularly depraved. Two grown men of God were forcing a young boy to masturbate them simultaneously or perform oral sex on one or both of them at the same time, or perform oral sex on one, while the other humped me from the rear. There was no limit to their depravity and torture, and their appetite to violently attack me. I could only mentally shut down until it was all over. For these windows of time, I simply did not exist. I had no mind, no heart, and no feelings. I was not a person. My tears and emotions had long since stopped flowing.

My mother's words rang loud and clear to keep me submissive and compliant. I never told a soul. The extent to which I was willing to endure this violence speaks volumes about my relationship with my father and the fear I held toward him. Although it happens less frequently, even today at age 68, there are moments when I can still feel the unspeakable pain of being penetrated.

As I look back on my abuse by the priests, I have come to believe that I was selected for sexual abuse and I was identified through the confessional. In school the nuns preached over and over about the importance of purity and the need to confess impure thoughts or actions. I believe the priests heard the naïve and innocent confessions of a young boy and used them to their own evil and devious advantage. I also see now that their manipulative behavior was done with practiced skill. This was not the first time for either of them and, I suspect, not the last time.

From the perspective of adulthood, I can see how the priests "groomed" my parents and me, and maybe others around us. Grooming is the process used by a predator to completely mute the warning signals and disarm the defense mechanisms of a child and those around them. The predators build friendship and trust with the adults and gently and methodically work to understand and meet the emotional and physical-affection needs of the intended victim. The sexualization of this relationship by the predator is a steady and calculated process. Before the victim even begins to understand what has happened, they feel involved, ashamed, and complicit.

Growing up in a house of emotional sterility, I was an obvious and easy candidate for abuse. The grooming skill of the predators, combined with my blind obedience to the directions of the nuns and other adults, resulted in my personal boundaries being easily crossed and my defenses disarmed. My mother placed complete and total trust in our priests, discounting any efforts on my part to avoid them or stop their involvement with me.

Another attempt I made to find safety while growing up was joining the Cub Scouts. It was fun, interesting and a safe diversion from real life. In time, I graduated to the Boy Scouts and hoped and prayed that it, too, would continue to be a safe haven where I could spend my time having some fun and adventures. The scout master was a close family friend so how could I go wrong? Everything was great in the beginning and I was excited as we headed out for my first camp experience. Unfortunately, this trip to Boy Scout Camp was to destroy any hope of safety or expectation of good times.

It started when the scoutmaster called me into his cabin. As I look back on that day, I see a small-statured, almost mousy-looking man with a whiny voice and a strong body odor smell about him. He told me I had to complete an initiation before he would allow me to be a full member of the troop. He said it was an important step that would show my commitment to him and the troop. I only had to do what he told me and I would be accepted forever. He added that the initiation was a secret process, and if I ever told anyone about it, I would be thrown out of the troop and branded a troublemaker. As he said it, I remembered my mother's threatening words about obedience.

He told me to kneel down in the middle of his bed, and I did. He told me to slide down my pants and underpants, and I did. He told me to repeat, "O what an ass I am," over and over and over again. When I said it quietly, he told me to speak up and say it loudly so that he knew I really believed it. I remember yelling those words as vividly as if it happened only yesterday. I no longer wanted to be a Boy Scout. He then started laughing at me and humiliating me for being so "tiny." He insisted I come close to him so that I could see what the real thing looked like. He unzipped his pants and removed his erection and put my hands on it. He then told me, "Someday, you will be a man, like me," and my Scout Master proceeded to do to me what predators do to little boys. This went on for over a year, and when I tried to quit scouts, I was told that "quitters never win and winners never quit." Through this whole experience I shed no tears and felt absolutely nothing.

My abuse was not to be limited to people I knew and trusted. I remember the day when a stranger first attacked me. I had stopped at the train station on my way home from school to use the rest room. It was a dingy and smelly place, but it was the only public bathroom on the way home. I put down my book bag and stepped up to the urinal to do my business. The next thing I knew, there was a large and tall man standing next to me. I didn't react because I recognized him as one of the clerks from behind the ticket counter. It never occurred to me that I was in danger. As I finished my business, I felt him put his hand on the back of my neck and squeeze firmly. With his other hand he took my hand and placed it on his penis and started to massage it. After he was finished, he brought my face down to it so it could "thank me." He rubbed it on my face and across my mouth, leaving a disgusting odor and his semen. He then zipped himself up and walked out. I washed my face, picked up my books and walked home, thinking that maybe the whole world was this way. I had no tears or rage left for what had just happened. Fortunately, he never approached me or spoke to me again, but my list of predators had grown.

Mixed among these evil–doers were three other men who sexually assaulted me. They included a man who gave me a ride when I was hitchhiking, a teen who exposed himself to me, and a doctor, who fondled me extensively while doing a physical. Because these events were less invasive, I have tended to place less importance on them. That probably highlights how distorted my boundaries were and how easily I accepted inappropriate behavior. It was as though I had a big sign on my forehead announcing that I was vulnerable and an easy target.

I don't remember when any of the abusers stopped violating me. I can only assume that, over time, the predators got tired of me or, worse, replaced me with other victims. I also do not remember when the real life events stopped being a part of my memory, but that clearly happened. From these early years until my early 50's, I had no conscious memory of the abuse. While the physical violence in my life stopped when the predators lost interest in me, the emotional damage continued on. My nightmares and dreams had become so vivid and the fear and distorted thoughts were so firmly implanted that I didn't need the physical events to feel abused any longer. The threats of exposure never stopped. The fear of my father and the lack of protection by my mother sealed my silence for decades.

4

MY FIRST HETEROSEXUAL EXPERIENCE

When I had my first heterosexual experience, it was early spring and I had just turned twelve. I remember sitting on a bed in a room at home and there were two other people in the room, a young man and a young woman. I knew them both and never considered that I could be at risk. They were laughing and talking and then at some point, he reached over and took hold of my hands, pulling me down onto my back. As he held me down across the bed, the woman started to tickle me and told me that that I was about to take my first step into manhood. She then unbuckled my pants, slid them down and removed my underpants. She started to massage my thighs and my genitals and kiss and suck on my penis.

My body instinctively knew only one reaction; it came alive and responded in ways I had not known possible. While I was filled with fear, there was an excitement about the physical experience. Soon, she removed her clothes and proceeded to straddle me and rape me. Her partner had been holding me down through the entire ordeal, and now he let my hands loose and put them on her breasts. He kept telling me the whole time that "you are now a real man." When they were finished with me, they told me to go take a shower and they left. Did real men feel so dirty and so scared?

There has been no event in my life more confusing than this one. I knew it was wrong, I knew I was being victimized, and yet, physically it felt good. I had no mental capacity to process what had happened. I felt dirty, disgusting, and responsible, but I wanted to do it again – I was in a state of tremendous conflict. The fact that it was not physically painful confused me in ways that took decades to resolve. At the time, I didn't understand the difference between physical pain and emotional pain/damage. For weeks afterwards, every time I made eye contact, I was overwhelmed with the fear that each person would somehow know of my secret life; it was written on my body.

5

A CHILD'S STRUGGLE TO SURVIVE

I lost my innocence at an early age. Afterward, there never was a time when my guard was not up and I was not constructing a lie or manipulating an event in order to find a safe place to exist. Emotional, physical, and mental isolation were my retreats, especially while I was living through abusive events. It was in those quiet and dark corners of my mind where I stayed until the violence was over. Afterward, I would take long showers in an effort to scrub off the smell and feel of the abuse. But there was not a soap strong enough or water hot enough to cleanse me.

While I could retreat to isolation and separation from others when I was awake, the night was not as kind to me. I remember a single terrifying and recurring nightmare that left me awake and scared in the middle of the night. It followed me everywhere I went, and well into adulthood. I realized many years later that what I thought was a child's nightmare was the real violence perpetrated on me and played out in my dreams for decades after the original events. I had developed an emotional numbness to seal off the memories in a deep and dark recess where they remained for decades, only to surface in the dark of the night. The damage was so significant that I simply suppressed all the details and was left with distorted values and a dysfunctional life.

I remember little about my childhood that doesn't include abuse. Along with my lost innocence came an abundance of pain, suffering, fear, insecurity, and sorrow. As I look back now, I wonder who I was and who I might have been had the abuse not occurred. I look at pictures from my early childhood and try to reconstruct myself from a few shards of memory, but I can't do it. I once saw gossip illustrated in a film as feathers in a pillow that has been cut open. The feathers fly everywhere, never to be gathered up and stuffed back into the pillow again. And that is the same as the lost innocence of an abused child. Nothing can bring it back after the deed is done. You may find little pieces of who you really were, some pieces of your innocence before all the evil, trauma, and fear entered you life, but reassembling the original person is not possible.

Pre-teen and teen years are important periods in the formation of a child's moral compass and value system. Parents and other adults convey most of this important information as they interact with the child everyday. But even daily Mass and church became dangerous. The priests who gave me communion or absolution were also penetrating me violently. I was told that it was a sin to tell a lie, but I learned that manipulation and lying were necessary to find safe moments away from the predators and avoid the ruthless hand of my father. I learned that sex, violence, coercion, and intimacy were all the same.

The pervasiveness of the abuse in my life caused me to sexualize everything, whether it was a word, a visual image, or physical contact – sex was my filter. It distorted the very foundation of my personal ethics and values.

As I got older, I realized that the "Ozzie and Harriet" image I had of my family and many of their close friends was a myth at best. For years, I thought we were special, characterized by us five boys sitting in a row at church or wearing our acolyte robes for the Christmas picture. The abuse, the fear, and the guilt were all part of the hidden life I led. I was a little boy and living a double life. What child can understand and sustain such duplicity without becoming confused and creating destructive patterns of behavior to cope? To keep your sanity you rationalize that what you are experiencing is normal and typical and that all your friends are experiencing the same things. In your double life, you are forced to present a smiling, cheerful and contented image to the outside world and to never allow anyone to see or know the dark side. The threats of retaliation from the perpetrators are so strong, and the fear of the iron hand of authority so frightening, there is no possibility of going to the authorities.

I spent many years stepping on and over the boundaries of others. In my childhood world, the boundaries I learned were much different than those boundaries that others seemed to live by. For years and years, I thought they had the problems. When I understood the reality, I thought I was literally going crazy. I had learned to be skeptical and untrusting of everyone. In every relationship, I looked for ulterior motives and expected deceit and manipulation. As a result, I used isolation as a safety net from the danger and harm I believed was all around me even as, especially as, an adult. Being open or transparent in any way might lead to exposure of the truth. It was not until a courageous victim of child sexual abuse by a priest spoke out and was interviewed on the national news that I began to understand the trauma of my past.

His disclosure helped me unearth the memories and I started to understand how distorted my personal boundaries were and how confused my concept of self and relationships was. I began to have flashbacks of my past abuse and began the difficult struggle to process that information and begin to heal.

I was always envious when I heard people talk about loving parents or warm and happy relationships with family and friends while growing up. I simply made up stories as a way of fitting in and not allowing my shadow-life to be exposed. My made-up world led to a broad selection of masks I could wear according to my need at the time. The skill to flip from mask to mask, or to modify a mask to deceive or manipulate, while all the time hiding my real identity, evolved naturally from an early age. I had so many masks, and moved easily from one to another, that at times I lost track of Tom Scales. At times I wanted to lose track of who Tom Scales was. Most of the time, I was who I needed to be at any given moment. I had learned to laugh on the outside, while crying or screaming with excruciating pain on the inside. The threats of the predators were so scary, that I carried them with me through my adult life. The predators had taught their lessons well.

6

NAVIGATING HIGH SCHOOL AND COLLEGE

Beginning with high school and continuing through college, I had developed skills that helped me avoid open and intimate relationships and the exposure of the real me. This process seemed to come naturally to me and I had no idea why relationships and openness were so scary for me. At the same time I worked hard to avoid predators. Since I could not tell a predator from a safe person, I simply avoided people in general. My survival was really isolation in an emotional cave. I could talk sports, weather, news, or business all day long. I could play bridge from dawn to dark, but anything personal rarely found the light of day. I studied long hours, and I played bridge and sports in order to keep busy at all costs.

Individuals typically put a lot of thought into the choice of their college majors, but I chose Wheeling College because I received a scholarship and I was told that, if I went there and chose chemistry as a major, I would be assigned a particular professor as my advisor, who would give me good counsel through college. So, even though I barely passed chemistry in high school, I went along with that advice. Doctor Bob Grob was, without question, one of the finest men I have ever met. As my advisor, and later as my friend, he was the first adult I felt I could trust who offered friendship without deceit or evil intent. He was a man of honor and integrity at an important time in my life. He seemed to sense my turmoil, although we had never discussed it. I learned by his actions that I did not need to fear all men and it gave me hope at a time when I desperately needed it.

As I got older and felt more isolated and confused about my mental and emotional turmoil, I began to pray I would die. If I scratched my leg or arm playing football, I hoped it would get infected and I would die from the infection. I could get a sinus infection or the flu and quietly hope and pray it was cancer or some other incurable disease that would end my suffering without me having to take the action to do it. Only God knows how many times I thought I had leukemia and the end was, hopefully, quickly coming. Many were the times when I looked at the wheels of a semi and hoped my car would take control and collide with the truck. Bob Grob's kindness and friendship helped me through those dark days.

The very fact that I spent so much time focused on dying and somehow ending my life was extremely stressful, primarily because I did not understand why I felt that way. All I knew at the time was that I was both fearful and scared.

My summers during college were spent alone. I painted houses by myself and made good money doing it. The work was boring. At the same time, I was going through changes that I simply did not see or understand. Looking back as an adult, I realize that it was during this period that depression became a part of my everyday life and fed the negative views I had of myself. I didn't understand why I felt this way or where these feelings came from. I also started seriously drinking. I realize now that the boredom of the work and the depression from childhood trauma drove me to find ways to numb my mind and my feelings. Alcohol was an obvious choice. House painting allowed me to pay my way through college and still have extra money to support my drinking. I frequently had a hangover, and I told my parents I thought the fumes from the paint were bothering me. Even though I was painting outside, they seemed to believe it, or they really didn't care. I used that excuse over and over. I painted from sun up to sun down, leaving little time for anything else.

In 1962, I was awarded an appointment to the United States Naval Academy, and once again, I thought my life was going to take a turn for the better. After one year of college, I left for the Academy. There was much I loved about academy life. It was physically demanding and included rigorous academic discipline. There was little time for the symptoms of my past to creep in. However, two issues kept nagging at me. I didn't understand my worries at the time, but I had first an inordinate fear of being in a place that was exclusively men, and second being in a place where the men were in absolute and total control. It became clear that allowing other men to have complete control over me was far too scary to endure for long. I knew I could not stay and the U.S. Navy was not a place where I could survive. In the end, my fear overcame my desire for a naval career and I left, returning to college and burying myself in course work.

I learned from my experience at the Naval Academy that there were certain situations, people (appearance and behavior), and circumstances that brought all the fears and anxiety to the surface, even though at the time I had no idea what the root cause was. I had repressed it all. Each time I felt this anxiety, I would find myself feeling as a child with no protection and a powerful voice taking control of me. It was worse than nightmares in many ways because it could happen in a class triggered by a teacher, or later, at work in a meeting triggered by a colleague or an executive. All my alarm bells would be going off to tell me I was in danger but I didn't know what the danger was. It all made no sense to me and there were many times I struggled to maintain my composure. I failed physical chemistry my junior year of college because of a visceral fear of the instructor. I simply could not think or function in his class.

When I returned to college from the Naval academy, I quickly restarted my drinking. The intense activity level at the Academy had taught me to maintain a constant and full schedule. As a result, I combined the numbing effects of alcohol with ridiculous academic loads in college leaving no time to be a person. One semester I took an impossible load of 30 credit hours – unheard of under any circumstances. With courses such as physics, organic chemistry, and calculus, I had little time for a social life. The following semester, I backed off and only took 26 credit hours. Without understanding why, I was deliberately creating isolation to avoid, as much as possible, interpersonal contact. It worked quite well, and I used this tactical crutch with practiced expertise throughout my adult work life.

I dreaded each day of college, feeling somehow more vulnerable and fearing that my secret would be discovered; I dated very little through high school and college, because I was afraid to allow people to come close to me. I remember one situation from high school when I believed I was completely and totally in love. However, with each interaction or conversation, fear and anxiety overtook me and I did everything I could to push her away. When that didn't work, I went quickly back into isolation. It is hard to look back and see how harshly

I behaved and how kind she was in spite of it all. The really difficult part for me was that I couldn't understand why I was unable to have a warm, close and comfortable relationship with someone I cared about, like others seemed to have.

I simply could not build and maintain a happy, healthy relationship. As I look back, I now see that getting past the fear of exposure and the dread of openness and vulnerability seemed to be insurmountable hurdles. The damage of my youth played over and over in every relationship I had. I learned that the value system by which I lived was different from others, but I didn't know how to change it. It was during this time that I started to watch other people carefully, trying to distinguish how to act and to understand what was wrong with me. It didn't work and I became more and more confused. I lived constantly with an anxiety of impending doom. No matter what good happened, I was always looking over my shoulder for the bad to follow quickly behind. This meant that I could never celebrate or enjoy accomplishments or recognition. I could get promoted at work on one day and be fearful the next day that I was going to be fired. I just knew the "evil me" would be exposed and my world would come crumbling down.

7

BUILDING A NEW FAMILY

Finding a mate was a difficult, almost treacherous, process for me. I had the emotional sensitivity of a fence post, so I could not really get to know any of the women I dated. During graduate school I moved into an apartment and started dating a girl in the adjacent apartment. This only lasted until I went to her place one afternoon, and as we were standing outside talking, her roommate, Liza, drove up in her 1962 Comet with red bucket seats and we were introduced. I still remember Liza's blond hair, her ballet-rehearsal outfit, and her smile. She was so petite, she wouldn't make a good paperweight and I wondered how she survived in a strong wind. It was not long after our meeting that I stopped by to see the woman I was briefly seeing, but she wasn't home from work yet. Liza invited me in to wait and we passed the time chatting while she started to make dinner. When her roommate came in, she took one look at us and went straight up stairs. She said later that she knew at that moment that we simply belonged together.

Looking back, I believe that it was the casual and easy way we could talk that first attracted me to Liza. We had a comfortable friendship, before romance entered in – a very new experience for me. As we got to know each other better, we found that we had almost nothing in common. She was too cute for words, trim, artistic, and a ballet dancer. I was overweight, a chemist, analytical to a fault, and clumsy at best on a dance floor. With all this going for us, we hit it off right away. Over the next few months we did our best to burn down the apartment building. First, we charred French fries in the oven and set it on fire. Then, not long after that, we fell asleep on the living room floor with candles burning. The candle holder was made of cast iron and we had set it on a newspaper to collect the dripping wax. We woke up to the sound of crackling flames and burning paper. The carpet was destroyed when we were finished, but only after Liza threw water on the flames and I grabbed the hot candle holder with my bare hand to throw it off the carpet onto the tile floor. We made a trip to the emergency room to learn that being burned by wax is antiseptic and we were sent home. These hot events were the kind I could handle. They were the foundation on which we have built 40 years of love, challenges, and adventures, and memories. We have been blessed with two wonderful children and one granddaughter.

Liza and I were married in March 1971. A time that should have been exciting and joyful became a sad restatement of the disdain my family had for me and their willingness to express it openly. They went out of their way to exacerbate my sense of disposability during this time. On one occasion, we were invited for dinner to celebrate our engagement (I believe the words were, "To welcome Liza into the family"), only to find that everyone had eaten and the food was nearly gone when we arrived. On another occasion, another brother invited us to a party to celebrate our engagement. We rushed home to have dinner after work before going. When we arrived at the party we realized that all the other guests had been invited for dinner. My mother threatened not to attend the wedding because she considered it an excommunicable sin to step foot into a non-catholic church, especially a Baptist Church. Last, I can still see clearly as my parents, brothers, and spouses all walked out of our wedding reception before we had even cut the cake. Wedding gifts from most of my brothers never arrived. The whole family seemed to take up the silent chant of my youth: "You are disposable and we couldn't care less about you." When I heard from one brother the words "I love you, but I don't have to like you," I assumed I was the cause of this behavior and deserved it all. I allowed these messages to reinforce all the negatives of my youth.

That I was unprepared to share my life with another person is the understatement of a lifetime. Although I was 28-years old, I was emotionally immature and had little concept of the responsibilities of marriage and partnership. Little did I realize that I had brought a backpack of dysfunction with me into our marriage. In retrospect I realize that my child sexual abuse was the prism through which I filtered all communication and judgments. I had no understanding about how to discuss or negotiate differences, and I had no idea what emotional intimacy was. I didn't know how to say, "I'm sorry," when I needed to apologize. My tendency was to fall back on the behavior I saw in my family growing up, an unhealthy path that took years to recognize and change. While I was learning, those closest to me were suffering.

There were so many times when I should have been the defender and protector of my wife, but I did not act. I was so accustomed to the depression and boundary issues from being physically and sexually abused, that even the most egregious behavior didn't seem wrong or out of line to me. As a result, I stood silently by. The fact that our marriage has survived 40 years is more a testimony to her patience and commitment than to my healthy participation.

When it came to parenting, I was even less prepared. The only models I'd had were my cruel father and my defensive and long-suffering, pious mother. I was either too lenient or too strict with my children; there was no middle ground. I was oblivious to events that should have captured my attention. I was a workaholic; after coming home late, I would hide behind the newspaper or television to avoid intimacy and interaction with my family.

I had no sense of the perspective that allowed me to make reasonable judgments about appropriate consequences for specific behaviors. Consistent with life patterns, I would isolate myself when unhappy and rationalize to myself that either everything was my fault or everything was someone else's fault. I had no middle ground for shared responsibility. Looking back, all of my childhood had taught me that I was the problem and if I just accepted responsibility, the conversation would end and the issue would go away. Tomorrow would be a new and better day. Resolving issues and conflicts were not in my skill set.

I also had a built in predisposition to my father's sullenness and quickness to anger. I could ignore the most obvious attacks or insults and respond emotionally and intensely to situations that I would later, with a clearer mind, see as trivial. Viewing life through my abuse gave me plenty of opportunities to get angry and I didn't miss many of them. Harnessing all that rage and frustration and using it for good would come later.

It was only through the courage of Frank Fitzpatrick, the brave man who publicly broke his silence about Father James Porter, the priest who abused countless children for many years in the Boston area, that

I was able to finally understand my life. My wife, daughter and I were sitting on the bed in our Boulder, Colorado home watching the news one night when Frank was being interviewed about his story. Somehow, listening to him talk opened my eyes to the events that took place in my frequent nightmares, and the turmoil of my life suddenly seemed so obvious and clear. It connected my dreams to my past and from that day a flood of repressed memories began to surface. They came at an overwhelming rate. This was about 1993 and I was 50-years-old. There had been many sleepless nights and long periods of self-hate and self-destructive behavior before the revelation of that evening.

I have never met Mr. Fitzpatrick, but his extraordinary courage was the first step on my path of healing. There are no words adequate to thank him for his valiant action and the positive impact it had on me, but I can and do thank him here and now.

8

THE SURVIVING IN THE WORKPLACE

Wearing masks is a way of life for a survivor of child sexual abuse. In many cases you do it subconsciously as part of the defense mechanisms you build. As an adult I became a practiced expert at being what others expected. I could be analytical and detached one minute and compassionate and thoughtful the next. The real issue was that this behavior was not genuine, it was all on the surface, and there was no feeling, no compassion, and no heart on the inside. It was an instinctively calculated measure of what was required of me at the moment. If this involved creating fiction, I created fiction. If it involved manipulating the truth, I manipulated the truth. Most importantly, it involved hiding my reality. I learned to smile when overwhelmed with sadness and I learned to laugh while suffering inside. For years I did not understand the source of these feelings and thought that they were normal. My masks helped me avoid the obvious questions that would come if others saw the real me. My masks gave me various personas that I could like and who represented the person I wished I was. I hated the real me and kept it subdued with alcohol as often as possible. For years, the contrast between the person inside and the person on the outside was striking.

I discovered that I could have a life style that allowed me almost total emotional isolation and yet seemed to be both accepted and appreciated by those around me. I simply changed jobs frequently, which fit well into my strategy to stay emotionally disconnected. I worked at a large pharmaceutical company in New Jersey early in my career and in my 20 years there, I had many different jobs. Most folks thought I was only climbing the ladder of success and in some ways I was, but I was also disconnecting from a place before people could get too close. I struggled with the mental and emotional gymnastics of excitement at success on the one hand and fear of discovery on the other. I simply had no idea how to build and sustain healthy personal relationships, so I tried to avoid situations where my flawed and damaged character would be highlighted.

Near the end of my tenure at the New Jersey company I took a 2 plus year assignment in Switzerland. It was a place where my desire and need for isolation were reinforced because solitude is a strong characteristic of the Swiss culture. Most employees had private offices and worked with their doors closed; they opened them only to go to lunch and to go home.

Initially, this felt like solitary confinement and I had trouble adjusting. However, as time passed the isolation suited me just fine. I could even leave my door open, knowing no one would ever venture in unless invited. The move to Switzerland was the first step in a long series of short-term jobs all done under the guise of consulting or built on the application of some special skills I thought I had. I was fortunate to have skills that allowed me to change jobs and I practiced them faithfully and regularly. While I had five different jobs in one company the first twenty years of my career, I worked for eight different companies at eleven different locations during the last sixteen years of my career. I traveled the world, literally, and never let anyone get too close. I believe that all of these job changes and apparent job instability were subconsciously created to be self-protective. During my career, I worked with thousands of people, shared offices and roles with many, and I need fewer than five fingers to count the people whom I could call today and have a friendly, or even a casual, conversation, much less identify them as my true friends.

I have come to realize that I had friends but my friends never had me. The real story of my life was deeply buried. Preventing someone from truly getting to know me was always my first priority. I had been told many times in life that if someone really gets to know me, they would not want anything to do with me. This message only reinforced the idea that there was something seriously wrong with me. I sense it, felt it and yet it wasn't until I heard Frank Fitzpatrick that I started to understand. I felt responsible for everything bad that happened and felt evil and dirty, without understanding why.

9

COLLATERAL DAMAGE

My interpretation of the words "collateral damage" means the unintended consequences of an event. In war, there is collateral damage when civilians are harmed or killed. If you don't really know how to treat people respectfully and your value system from youth teaches you to be a taker, self-driven, and not giving or compassionate, the effect is that you cause harm to many around you along the way, even those who are closest to you and love you. Sadly, in many cases you may not even know you are doing it, or worse, you know you are doing it and you don't seem to be able to stop yourself. You are interacting with others using the norms and values formed during your violent childhood and, at the same time, you trust that your parents, your priests, and others have taught you properly and modeled appropriate behavior. In my case nothing could have been farther from the truth. The most obvious place for this damage to happen is within your family. How you parent, how you build the father-son or father-daughter relationship – these are all created with the trauma of your youth as a foundation. Being close, loving, and supportive when you never saw that behavior in action is difficult at best.

One of the most difficult steps for me came after I understood my abuse and needed to talk with my children. Sitting with each one and explaining as best as I knew what had happened and how I thought it had impacted me was the easy part. Talking about how the behavior I modeled for them and stating the fact that I had never taken my abuse to the next generation, was enough to make me sick inside. However, it was a conversation that needed to take place, maybe as much for me as for them. While talking with each of them, their reactions taught me wonderful lessons about unconditional love.

In the early 1990s, I was having a lot of medical problems with no conclusive diagnosis. I discussed this with my mother and she made a surprising suggestion. "Thomas, you need to be tested for AIDS." Nothing could have shocked me more because I didn't think she even knew what AIDS was, much less how one got it. I assured her that I had no association with the two known causes of IV drug use and a homosexual lifestyle. She repeated this to me three more times and seemed determined that I get tested. I didn't. As the realities of my abuse began to unfold, I realized that my mother had known about it for many years and had never taken any action on my behalf. I believe these few sentences about AIDS were her way of trying to tell me about my past and the inherent risks from what had happened to me. Just as I carried my secret, she also carried hers and it gnawed at her through the latter years of her life. I have no doubt that she was damaged by my abuse. She must have told some family members, because distant relatives actually told me about my abuse, not realizing in some cases that they were filling in pieces of the puzzle I did not have. I got some subtle and not so subtle signals that many in the family knew about what had happened to me but no one lifted a finger to help me. That word "disposable" popped back in my mind. The damage caused when adults do not step forward and protect a child at risk, or simply turn their heads and ignore a dangerous situation, adds a new and compounding measure of trauma to the survivor.

There was a second important interaction with my mother that would leave me burdened. After I came to understand a lot about my abuse I talked briefly with her about it on the phone. She then visited us in Boulder, knowing specifically that I wanted to discuss it with her. She came for a week and after a couple of days relaxing and seeing the local sites, we sat in the family room one evening and I started the discussion. I tried to use gentle words and not be in any way accusatory. I was looking for understanding and I hoped a little compassion. I was also looking for pieces of the puzzle that would help me heal. After just a few minutes she looked me square in the eye and said, "Thomas, you just need to forget about this and go on with your life."

You could have knocked me over with a feather. I told her that I did not have that choice, because the abuse had so damaged me that I had to deal with it, find a way to heal, and then move on. Left alone, it would only gnaw at my insides to the end of my days. She cut her visit short leaving early the next morning and she never came back again. For the last time she had a chance to choose me, to support me, and to help me heal, but she chose not to.

Collateral damage also happens in work relationships as you manipulate your way to bigger jobs, which means more work, and in turn means a bigger protection zone from real relationships. It can happen in personal relationships when you have pliable or inappropriate personal boundaries. As a result, you tend to be close when you should be distant and distant when you should be close. You frequently allow others to set the tone of a relationship, regardless of how that tone presents itself and how it makes you feel. You assume friendship where there is none, and you treat your friends poorly because you don't understand the meaning of true friendship and how to share an honest, healthy relationship with another person. My wife would ask me how I felt about a sermon at church and I accused her of trying to put me down because I wouldn't have the right spiritual answer. Or she would ask me how I felt about something – anything – and I told her I wasn't thinking anything. I had no opinions or I would change my opinions according to how she (or others) expressed hers. I felt threatened while at the same time I had no feelings to convey.

On a relational basis, I was without a doubt the classical "bull in the china shop." My actions at times ranged from ignorant to harsh to obnoxious. I found myself manipulating situations even when to do so was unnecessary and irrelevant. I had a fine-tuned skill for lying, honed to avoid the physical and emotional abuse of my father and the sexual abuse of the predators. The tendency was to see the other person as the problem, regardless of how kind or helpful they had been, then disconnect and move on. On many occasions I saw kindness and generosity as weakness. I couldn't understand how anyone could let others get so close or try to get so close to me. While I envied those kind and soft-spoken people, I had no idea how to act that way. Changing my behavior would require a certain level of introspection and honesty and, for decades, I simply was not capable of it.

There certainly were many moments in my life that I would choose to take back and relive with the value system that I hold dear today.

10

THE STRUGGLE TO HEAL

Healing is a challenging and difficult path. A survivor needs to break their silence, before the process can start. That in itself felt very risky at the time. The next step is equally important, and that is that the survivor must make a firm and personal commitment to honesty and integrity. As a result of the abuse, a survivor learns many compensation mechanisms to avoid detection, exposure, conflict, criticism, and harsh aggressiveness. You do or say whatever is necessary to achieve this end. This has to change for true healing to take place. A key aspect of this step is the willingness to take full responsibility for your words and actions. In order to heal, you can no longer cast all the blame on your past. This does not mean one should not pursue justice for the crimes committed. But it does require an honest and candid view of one's self. It means transparency inward and with others.

When we lived in New Jersey, and before I understood about my child sexual abuse, I started going to counseling. I didn't think I needed it, but my emotional ups and downs were obvious to everyone but me. I went at my wife's persistent requests. Looking back, I need only to have a candid view of my father to understand what it was like to live with me during those years. To me, the turmoil was normal and something I had experienced internally all my life. It really became a problem when others could see it clearly and it had an impact on their lives.

During that time in counseling I learned that I could actually make some choices about who I was and how I acted. This was a thought that had never occurred to me. After leaving New Jersey and experiencing the disclosure by Frank Fitzpatrick, I sought out more counseling and tried to find professionals experienced in treating people with my background. Over the years, I have worked with seven or eight different counselors and each has made a contribution to my healing. After all that counseling, I had surfaced many ugly memories and had analyzed them to death. I had written about them and written letters to my perpetrators. Nothing seemed to lance the emotional boils and allow them to heal. I also realized that I had probably surfaced only the tip of the iceberg of my child abuse. The sexual abuse was so pervasive and so violent, that I didn't realize that I needed to spend at least as much time and effort dealing with the emotional and physical abuse as I did on the acts of sexual abuse.

My sexual abuse as a child left me terrorized by the prospect of an intimate relationship with a woman. As a result, I walked away from many opportunities for relationships. Facing the expectation that I would never find a mate that would want me, I went to a prostitute in Amsterdam on my first trip to Europe. When I told my wife about it before we married, I explained that it had been out of curiosity of sex because growing up Catholic, I was taught that sex before marriage was a sin. I told her that as a grown man, I had wanted to face the fear I had of intimacy and sex. This experience was at best unsatisfying and I left wondering what could have possessed me to do it in the beginning. The woman's words to me as I left were insightful: "It is different when you love the person you are with."

Without question, the frequency with which men sexually violated me caused me to wonder if I was homosexual. Anytime I heard conversations that denigrated homosexual behavior, it caused me to draw tight the masks and barriers around me to be certain I was protected from discovery. When a pastor would preach on biblical themes related to homosexuality, I would cringe with the thought that maybe he was talking about me. For years I found contact with other men to be repulsive and avoided anything more than a handshake. Because of the jobs I had, I never wore jewelry, specifically a wedding ring. When I took a job in Atlanta and was living in a hotel and eating many of my meals in restaurants, I realized that more and more, men would end up hanging around my table. At work there were times when I had to keep a chair between certain male employees and me so they would not encroach on my personal space and boundaries. The situation was painfully obvious. After I bought a wedding ring, the unwanted advances seemed to stop – thank God.

Another phase of the impact of the child sexual abuse on my adult life came when I retired. Having used my job and constant travel as hiding places for years, I now felt fully exposed. With nothing to occupy my time and with little, if any, purpose to my life, the real depression set in. I was determined not to return to work. I spent the time playing word games, reading novels, exercising, and trying to come to terms with my life and myself. I closed myself off from my wife and children. I questioned that if this was all it was going to be, then maybe I needed to find a way out.

Throughout most of my adult life I had always gone back to one scripture, when life seemed intolerable. I was Psalms 31: 9-10.

> [9] Be merciful to me, LORD, for I am in distress;
>   my eyes grow weak with sorrow,
>   my soul and body with grief.
> [10] My life is consumed by anguish
>   and my years by groaning;
>   my strength fails because of my affliction,
>   and my bones grow weak.

These verses captured the hopelessness and pain I felt as I begged for God to intervene in some way on my behalf. As my healing progressed, these words would give me a deeper understanding and sense of empathy that allowed me to relate to other survivors in a most personal way. All things do work for good.

For years I had felt like a character out of The Wizard of Oz searching for a heart. I would be asked how I felt about a person, a picture, a color, a pattern, an event or just about anything else and I couldn't answer. I never thought about things around me; they just "were." I had no noticeable emotions or emotional reactions. If I ventured to offer an opinion and it was criticized, I took it personally. My opinion wasn't flawed or different – I was flawed.

To compensate, I watched what other people liked and mimicked their opinion. Sometimes I would express an opinion and soon after express the opposite opinion. My family would question me about my inconsistent views, and my response was always the same:

"Can't a person have a change of heart?"

Underlying all this was the fact that I FELT very little. I didn't feel pain. I didn't feel joy. I didn't feel happiness. I could not appreciate joyful moments, success, art, or beauty. What I did feel were anger and rage and I let my family feel the seepage as I tried to suppress those feelings. For me, happiness was not feeling rage.

My wife would ask me to follow through on something, and I perceived her request as criticism and a personal attack. Yet, when I didn't support her in a way that I had promised related to a particular situation, I made light of or ignored her pain and disappointment in me. I either never saw it or didn't see it as important.

While tears came easily, as a result of the early stages of abuse and the excruciating pain that came with it, after a time, they were all gone and nothing could cause my emotions to flow or show. Throughout most of my life, I have expected pain and sorrow, believed I deserved it, and was rarely disappointed.

As the extent of the damage from my youth became clearer, I began to look for ways and places to heal. Being raised in the Roman Catholic Church where I experienced abuse, I knew solace and healing were not possible there. In addition, the Catholic Church seemed to dedicate its energy and resources to protecting the predators. Even today, you don't see the church taking the known predators with all the evidence available and turning them in for prosecution. This would force the predators to take responsibility for the horrific damage they have caused to so many. The church might then have some credibility when it reaches out (if it ever truly does) to help the victims or protect children. All the financial judgments in the world do not heal the deep wounds of child sexual abuse. To my dying day, I will never understand this incredibly heartless and immoral position of the Roman Catholic Church; it is counter to anything I understand to be Godly or biblical.

I accepted Jesus Christ as my Lord and Savior in 1983 and waited patiently for Him to transform me. But that was not to happen either. My faith was shallow because I could not accept the love of anyone, much less a "Father." Life felt like it was two steps forward and three backward. I could never see progress and when I did, I was looking over my shoulder for some evil to pounce on me the minute I let my guard down. It was decades before I stopped this pattern of negative programming that kept me focused on the impending doom that I expected would follow any and all positive events in my life.

Over the following years, I went to various Bible studies; men of strong personal character mentored me, and I tried to surround myself with men of integrity. All of this was in the hope that God would somehow use the Bible or these men to transform and deliver me from the dark and dank dungeon where I lived. Nothing seemed to work and the more I tried the less success I had. The one constant feeling was inadequacy. I did not belong among such people. It was frequently embarrassing to be in the same group because they seemed to believe what they said, and they could comfortably and easily quote a scripture for any need, while I was just mouthing words. I felt "judged" but knew I deserved it. Under my thin skin was a filthy and evil person.

With my Catholic upbringing, I had read the New Testament over and over again. However, the messages of the Bible were so starkly different from my reality that I could never absorb them as principles for my life. The Scriptures seemed fake and I had only to look back at my experience with priests to reinforce that perspective. How could one believe the Bible when the specially chosen and ordained servants of God could behave in such devious and ruthless ways?

I read books on child sexual abuse and what others had experienced. I read about the problems and challenges similar to those I faced on a daily basis. I found little, if anything, that actually addressed the issue of healing. The professional counselors I saw over the years helped me gain some insight into the impact of the abuse and how it had molded me. But there also, studying the problem and unearthing additional disgusting memories did little to guide me to a healing path.

11

FINDING A PATH

With retirement and me face-to-face, new challenges surfaced quickly. The first eighteen months after leaving my last job were wasted. I constantly wondered if there was any constructive purpose for the rest of my life. Eighteen months is a long time when you are doing nothing with your days. Over and over my family expressed their concern and kept suggesting I go back to work, but I knew that was no longer an option. I repeatedly answered and believed wholeheartedly that I needed a new path for my life; I didn't know what it was, but I knew I would recognize it when I saw it.

Compounding my emotional turmoil was that a few years before I retired, I had some serious heart problems. It was a wake- up call that life is fragile and I had better make the most of it. When you believe you are facing death, it is a sobering experience. It causes you to begin looking at your life and assessing your value – you ask yourself over and over what you have contributed to the world.

I concluded that if I had died that day, only a mid-sized car would be needed to transport all the people who would come to a memorial service and mourn my passing. Somehow this seemed wrong and not a legacy I wanted to leave behind. I decided that my future efforts must do more to help others than all the years of my career. I needed a cause for which I held passion and one where my skills and abilities could be applied. I wanted to have an impact on the world before I left it.

Going through this thought process brought me peace and a certain degree of hope. I knew what I wanted, I had a sense of what it looked like, but I just had no idea where to find it. The most important clue came from a surprising place. While I had accepted the Lord in 1983 and attended church regularly, I never really prayed for anything but safety and protection – and those didn't come. I had bargained with God throughout my life, only to feel He didn't uphold His part of the deal, as I had wanted. My negotiating consisted of: "If You will….., then I will….." Looking back, it is not surprising that He did not respond. But I began one more time to reach out to God and pray that He would intervene in my life and turn it into something meaningful, useful, satisfying, and pleasing to Him. I made a commitment to myself that I would not just attend church regularly, but that I would use that time to pray, seriously consider the messages I heard, and try to find guidance that would move my life in a more valuable way. I decided I would not prejudge anything and be open to everything.

I knew that something good was going to happen, I sensed it, and it encouraged me to continue the search. The pieces began to fall in place in late April 2009; I was 66-years-old. One Sunday that April, I was sitting in church before the service and reading the bulletin, when one item jumped off the page at me:

> "Support Group for Adult Survivors of Child Sexual Abuse-
> 1st and 3rd Tuesdays each month at 7pm in Room 303."

It almost took my breath away. Was it possible there were others like me, buried in shame, guilt and self-hate? Not realizing it, I was facing one of my last barriers to true healing. I carried the bulletin around for six weeks before I found the courage to attend. My wife encouraged me to go because she believed that being with people who had my experiences would validate my life – we would all speak the same language and relate to each other in unique ways.

The night I finally decided to attend, I sat in the parking lot and waited until the very last minute to walk in, bringing a number of preconceived notions with me. First, I would be the only guy there and that would be embarrassing. How could I admit by simply walking in the room that I had been sexually abused? Would someone I know see me sitting in the group and quickly know my secret? Would there be only women there? How could I possibly talk in front of a group of women? How could I listen to what they had to say? If it were all women, how could they possibly help me? What value could my story be to them? If I opened my mouth and talked, would my world come crumbling down causing my life to never be the same again?

I walked into the room and was shocked to see four men and four women. None of them looked morose or suicidal as they smiled and introduced themselves. At best this took me off guard. Angela Williams, founder and co-moderator of the support group introduced herself and welcomed me. Jack Morgan the other co-moderator did the same. While I was happy to be there, I felt a certain tension in the room that gave me some angst. I took a seat in the circle and began quickly to ease my chair backwards. If there hadn't been a wall behind me, I might have backed into the next room. I kept my legs crossed and my arms folded in the polite, but highly protective position. I was petrified.

The normal routine is that when new people join the group, everyone in attendance tells their story and the new person has the opportunity to do the same. There were nine people including me, and I assumed that if I spoke I would go last. While they prayed for each other, I prayed we would run out of time before my turn came. Then Angela told us to take our time and not feel rushed and that we would take all the time necessary giving everyone a chance to speak – even if we had to stay late. We were free to speak or not, there was no pressure.

Listening to the stories was one eye-opening experience after another. All of a sudden I was not alone; I understood exactly what they were saying AND feeling. As they talked, I realized that some had far worse experiences than mine, physically and emotionally. Some had full recollection of their abuse and others were just starting to fill in the gaps. The common thread was that the damage seemed to be uniformly the same. The inability to trust others as adults seemed to plague all of us, regardless of the extent of the abuse. The failure of family and friends to acknowledge the abuse and take protective action when it occurred was the case in all situations that evening. This failure seemed to exacerbate the suffering and damage each individual suffered.

I had heard adults say frequently that: "I would kill (or some such similar violent word) any person who threatened or hurt my child." While the words were always bravely stated, the reality was that, in most cases, the adults meekly retreated and allowed the destruction of a child's innocence to happen unimpeded. Avoiding embarrassment was more important. Avoiding confrontation was more important. Avoiding exposure of a family member or friend who was a predator was more important. Except for the fact that predators do different things to little girls than they do to little boys, there was an amazing consistency of turmoil, emotional distress, isolation, shame, guilt and self-destructive behavior among all the participants that night.

Before I knew it, over an hour had passed and Angela was offering me the opportunity to speak. I did. I have no idea what I said that night. However, I did realize that it was the first time I had ever talked about my childhood sexual abuse in front of strangers – the first time I had talked about it in front of people who were not somehow bound to silence either professionally or because of other circumstances.

While I have no idea what I specifically said, I clearly remember the impact on me. After Angela prayed and everyone stood to leave, I felt like I was leaving hundreds of pounds of baggage in that room, never to be picked up again. I also knew that I would never view my abuse in the same way again – the guilt, the shame, the evil – they all belonged to the predators. I realized that night that I had been allowing people who, in some cases, had been dead for twenty years or more to have an impact on and control over my life today. It had to stop. I knew as I left that night that only one of my preconceived notions would become a reality – my life would never be the same again. I saw a glimpse of light at the opening of my cave, I liked what I saw, and I had no intention of retreating.

As we walked out, Angela offered to buy me a cup of coffee the next morning. We agreed to meet at a local coffee shop. She was ordering coffee as I walked into Biscuits & More and she stepped forward and gave me a big hug. She hugged – I panicked. I was not prepared for the idea that healing meant I had to have physical contact with other people.

We talked for over an hour and I was fascinated. I had never met anyone so open and candid about something I had dedicated so much energy to hiding. Our discussion covered both of our stories of abuse and the struggles we had dealt with to shed the self-destructive and compensating behaviors created for survival. We talked about the masks we used and the self-destructive behaviors we had survived. We talked about how certain individuals or certain situations triggered old mental tapes that put us back in those abusive situations and reversed the progress we had made in healing. The commonalities between our stories were surprising.

We talked a lot about VOICE Today, Inc., the non-profit she had founded, and her goals to break the silence and cycle of child sexual abuse and to encourage and support the healing of adult survivors. She covered the statistics generated by the Center for Disease Control in Atlanta, most of which I had never considered or known. It was stunning to hear that one in four girls will be sexually molested before the age of eighteen. Even more shocking is that one in six boys will also be molested before their 18th birthdays. All of my alarm bells went off when she told me that 90% of these victims would be abused by people they know and trust, and in many cases, love. My life seemed to confirm each statistic and reinforced the new idea that I was not alone. I thought about the affection I had felt for some of my abusers, the reverence I held for the priests, the respect I had for my Scout Master, and how distortions were created between love and trust and abuse. Her determination to break the silence and the cycle of child sexual abuse was infectious and I knew right away that THIS was what I had been looking for. VOICE Today and Angela's vision to change the world would become my vision, as well, and my mission and passion.

One thing in particular that Angela said gave me a new perspective on my life. It was very simple. I did not need to just survive my abuse, but I could have victory over my abuse, and in the process of claiming victory, I could also experience joy, inner peace, and true friendships. There was no need or reason to continue hiding. She gave me a copy of her book, From Sorrows to Sapphires Incest, Silence & God and I agreed to call her after I read it. I completed the 300-page book in less than a day.

The impact of Angela's book affected me immediately. I was stunned that a woman could write a story that seemed to recount my life so accurately. Except for the details of each abusive event, she had captured the shame, guilt, self-hate, isolation, confusion, and self-destructive behaviors that had been my life. During the course of our conversation, and in her book, one theme stood out: "You need to truly break your silence."

While I had talked openly and candidly at the support group and with Angela, it felt like there was an implied confidentiality in those discussions. These people would not speak openly about my abuse – that was my responsibility and my job. The fear, shame and guilt were things that I desperately wanted to shed. To really heal, I needed to stop being ashamed of my life and being fearful. To do that, I had to speak openly and freely about the harm done to me. Speaking out was an important step in transferring the responsibility and accountability for the abuse directly onto the predator. I would own none of it from that day forward.

As time passed, I became more interactive with the support group. Sharing was a healing experience as we all learned from each other. Discussions covered a wide range of topics and were adapted to the challenges that one or more of us were facing at the time. As one struggled, we all learned and we all contributed. It was a first step in rebuilding our trust of others. The individuals in the support group have become very special friends and there is a bond like none I have ever known before. I thank God for the wisdom, insight, and compassion they have contributed to my life and to me.

12

APPLYING MY TALENTS

Shortly after that coffee with Angela, I joined VOICE and began to take an active role to stop the abuse of children and support the healing of survivors. In the beginning, I spent a lot of time organizing our efforts and activities, structuring the VOICE programs and developing initiatives that simplified what we did and how we did it. Angela was frazzled, stretched thin, and tired from trying to do everything and be all things to all people. She was so giving, that everyone wanted her time, her ear, and part of her energy. We spent the first months figuring out what needed to be done, what the priorities were, and then how to divide up the work.

The volunteer team was loyal and capable, but because they were volunteers, we were able to get only a portion of their discretionary time. To create a clearer focus for VOICE, we talked about future plans and projects that we wanted to pursue and transformed them into a five-year strategic plan, which laid out what VOICE would be, what values would guide our activities and what strategic initiatives we would pursue. The back-up details for the strategic plan described the workshops, educational tools, and programs we planned on launching or improving. Many of those projects are a reality today. God had given Angela a vision for VOICE and we worked diligently to stay true to that vision.

When I joined VOICE, we had two workshops, both of which were dedicated to prevention. One was Stewards of Children 7-Steps to Prevent Child Sexual Abuse and the other was Internet Safety 101. It was Angela's vision that we build education into our prevention programs and use the workshops to train adults how to protect children. Our first step was to add two new workshops: Tough Talk to Tender Hearts and Time To Heal.

Tough Talk to Tender Hearts is a biblically-based program created by VOICE that teaches adults how to have a lifetime of age-appropriate conversations with children about healthy sexuality and personal boundaries, learning how to protect children, and empowering children to protect themselves. The program provides suggested topics for discussion, identifies teachable moments when a situation can provide an opportune time to talk about an issue or information in a relaxed way, and it provides scripts and age-appropriate language for children of all ages. It includes discussion points to teach a child and an adult how to respond appropriately when someone crosses those personal boundaries.

Time to Heal was created as an outreach to adult survivors of child sexual abuse, and it serves that purpose well. This workshop is also scripturally-based and has been demonstrated to be an effective program for survivors to learn about the impact of the abuse, to learn God's plan for their lives, and to begin the path of healing. In addition, it is a wonderful educational tool for the friends and family of adult survivors and can give them valuable insights into the challenges and issues a survivor faces along the path to healing.

Since those early days, VOICE has added:

The Grooming Mystery: A workshop designed to educate adults about the behaviors of predators and the actions and language that should raise alarms. Predators look like everyone else. One must understand the behavior of a predator to recognize impending risks and to be prepared to protect a child.

The Divorce Dilemma: A workshop designed to educate adults about the unique risks a child faces when a family is in crisis leading up to divorce, during the negotiation process, and in the single parent environment. This workshop is particularly important for other adults around the family in crisis, since the child may not be adequately supported or cared for by the parents. Children of divorcing and divorced parents are easy prey for a predator.

Survivor Struggles In The Workplace: A survivor of child sexual abuse graduates high school/college and gets a job. This workshop provides valuable information for the adult survivor and colleagues of the adult survivor to help them understand (1) how behaviors are learned during, and as a result of, the abuse, (2) how behaviors resulting from abuse can impact workplace relationships and success, and (3) key elements the survivor should keep in mind as they interact at work, and (4) how to help the survivor to minimize negative effects on personal and professional relationships, and career plans, while sustaining the healing process.

Cherished and Choices: These two workshops are designed for children and parents to attend together and highlights (1) how precious a child is in God's eyes, and (2) how God has a plan for each child and his or her body.

In addition, our healing and restoration programs now include an effective Support Group Program with a study guide. The study guide provides suggested discussion topics with thought-provoking questions to encourage candid discussion. VOICE also offers retreats that minister specifically to adult survivors of child sexual abuse. In 2010, this retreat was for women only, but in 2011, VOICE plans to sponsor an additional retreat for men.

VOICE has grown from just three workshop facilitators to fifteen. In addition to the United States, our workshops have been presented in Mexico and Eastern Europe and are scheduled for introduction in Africa in 2012. In 2009 we presented twenty workshops and in 2010 we presented over sixty-five. We have seen attendance at workshops more than triple over the same period.

13

STEPS THAT REINFORCED THE HEALING

For me, the support group was a place where I could finally talk openly about the dark corners of my life, put them in proper perspective, and then leave them behind. I cannot undo the abuse and I cannot reclaim my innocence, but I can and do have joy and peace in my life today. I have also established strong personal boundaries. As this process unfolded, I could feel the changes taking place. People would tell me that I was standing taller and smiling more. With each passing day, I felt better and better about myself. This empowered me to take more aggressive steps to heal.

One major change was the ability talk openly to anyone who asked such questions as," What do you do?" or "Are you retired?" My answer changed from, "Not much, I am retired," to "I work with a non-profit organization called VOICE Today." Almost on cue, people ask, "What do they do?" or "How did you get connected to them?" or "Why do you do that?" Those questions became easy segues into my testimony. The more I talked, the easier it got and the easier it got, the more I talked. I also learned that the message might need to take two or three or even four steps to reach the right person. We might give a copy of Angela's book to a person today and in a week or two, have a different person call and say, "Someone gave my friend Angela's book. Do you have some time to talk?"

Concurrently there was another transformation taking place. While my faith had been stagnant for years, I was now among people who had strong faith and in whose lives I could see it lived out each day. I was also much more open and receptive to listening, hearing and learning. This began to renew my trust in God and to help me disconnect the abuse by the priests from my view of God as Father. For the first time in my life, I did not feel dirty, filthy or unworthy. While in the past I could never come to terms with Romans 8:28, which states: "All things work for good for those who love the Lord and are called according to his purpose." I was beginning to see how my abuse was being transformed from a debilitating evil that kept me in a dark and self-destructive place to a talent in the biblical sense. The parable of the talents starting in Matthew 25:14 illustrates how important it is to use the resources and skills we are given to good purpose. The experiences I have had as a victim, survivor, and victor over the trauma of child sexual abuse are talents, and God has provided me a forum to effectively use them.

It was confusing that for years I felt too dirty and damaged to be baptized, when the very act of baptism is symbolic of a cleansing process. But my new chapter of healing set me free from the prison of guilt and shame and I was baptized at Johnson Ferry Baptist Church on November 1, 2009. I had now taken another important step in my healing and I knew that with each step, the possibility that I would fall back to the old me became less and less.

My relationship with God was growing, my relationship with trusted friends was growing, and my ability to distinguish acceptable from unacceptable behavior had taken on a quality I never thought possible. For the first time in my life I felt good about myself, I felt joy in my heart, and I enjoyed being around people. My relationship with my adult children was more open and honest than ever before. My marriage was becoming stronger and my ability to talk and discuss, but not be offended at the slightest comment, had improved communications and given new vitality to our relationship. I believed that my life had found a real and important purpose.

I found myself talking with more individuals struggling to heal which caused me to realize the true "value" of my child sexual abuse. The more I spoke out candidly about my abuse, the more people were willing to talk with me about their abuse. I found that my willingness to discuss in an open forum the changes I saw in my life, from the angry and rage-filled survivor unable to interact effectively with others on a day to day basis, to the transparent person willing to share about those evil acts, their impact on my life and how I was healing, gave others the courage to speak out, ask questions, and begin to heal. Shining light on the secrets and the abuse destroyed any hold those predators, their actions, and their threats had on me. My goal now is to show others that they can feel the same joy, happiness, and friendship that I experience.

Today I am the Executive Director of VOICE Today, Inc., a role that I take seriously and which gives me enormous personal satisfaction. I thank God each day for showing me the way to healing through VOICE. I have been blessed with the opportunity to talk with hundreds of survivors of child sexual abuse. Words cannot describe how wonderful it feels to use those horrible years of my life to help a survivor get past one the hurdles we all face in our healing. It is even more thrilling to see many of them heal and begin to minister to other survivors.

As I talk with each of them, I also can feel my healing growing and my faith strengthening. To be a part of this process, I have had to step far outside my original comfort zone – that emotional cave. I have to be open, transparent, and willing to share first. The very process of speaking out, without shame or embarrassment, about being sodomized, forced to do disgusting things, or having disgusting things done to me, enables other survivor to do the same. It seems like we all need to see that someone else can and will stand up and speak out and not be struck by lightening or have his or her life crumble. These steps into the light and toward openness and transparency can help destroy any strength the predator's threats have over the victim.

We are learning from each other. I find that my horrible years are packed full of experience and insight that help me share and minister to others, as Angela and the support group have ministered to me. Who better to write prevention programs about "grooming" than one who has experienced the process and can look back now as an adult and see all the signals missed or ignored by adults. Who better to talk about the emotional isolation and struggles with intimacy than one who has lived those struggles? Who better to talk about the triggers that caused the negative programming implanted by the predators to replay than a person who has traveled that path?

This is in no way meant to suggest that I feel completely "healed." Each day continues to be another step forward. I have rebuilt my personal boundaries and am better equipped to see more clearly when anyone starts to inappropriately cross those boundaries – including myself.

I know that God has both a plan and purpose for my life and He has made it abundantly clear. I work diligently each day to allow Him to use me to reach others rather than try to be the master of my own fate. I have found a patience I never realized I had, that allows me to work with others without imposing my own ideas, plans, or timelines. Sharing my story and sharing my path for healing allows them to take what is useful for them and make it part of their healing. People heal differently and at a pace suitable for their own needs.

I have also found that all those job changes, international travel, assignments, and organizational responsibilities of my professional career were a perfect training ground for what I currently do with VOICE.

14

FORGIVENESS

As I have struggled with the aftermath of my abuse through these past twenty years or so, I have replayed some scenarios over and over. The common theme was: "How could I bring life-changing harm to each of my predators and yet avoid the personal consequences of my action?" The answer came down to deciding if I was willing to risk my entire life, family, and future to extract some measure of revenge. Planning my own form of justice for these predators was a way of venting the deep and violent anger I felt. In the end I always concluded that avenging the evil done to me through physical violence would only leave me with blood on my hands and little, if any, satisfaction. It could not help me reclaim my life. The loss of my family was much too high a price to pay. I also came to realize that forgiveness is most powerful when you hold the tools of vengeance and destruction in your hand, and lay them down.

As my healing progressed, these thoughts haunted me less and less. I understand now that I do not know the full context of others' lives. Why did they act as they did? What experiences did they have that led to the insidious behavior? My conclusion was that only God knows the full story about each of my predators and their judgments are not my responsibility; they are His. I rest confidently that Jeremiah 17:9-10, which states: "I the Lord will search the heart and examine the mind, and judge a man according to his deed, according to what his actions deserve" will be applied to my life AND to theirs.

I have also come to properly understand forgiveness. Forgiveness is like love. For it to have true meaning and value, it must be given freely and without expectations of anything in return. I have freely and unconditionally forgiven the individuals who attacked me and changed my life forever. I pray that God in His infinite mercy will bring them to their knees in confession for what they have done to me, and most likely, to others. I leave their justice and restoration in His hands because I am certain that true forgiveness and internal peace cannot all share the same space with rage driven vengeance.

Letting go of this particular aspect of my rage has opened the door to more healing. My heart has become softer allowing me to feel in ways that were not possible before. No longer am I ashamed when I look in a mirror and see an image much like my father's. Today I am keenly aware of any behavior I learned under his tutelage and I work patiently to change it. My goal is to break the generational cycles and negative childhood programming that may still be having an impact on my life today.

Not expounding at length about my process of coming to a place of forgiveness might imply to some that finding the heart to truly forgive was an easy and painless process. Nothing could be farther from the truth. Forgiveness was one of the last pieces of my healing to fall into place. I struggled and bargained with God for years, wanting to have some say in how He would administer final justice. In the end, I fell back on the simple message that if I wanted God to forgive me, as I was forgiving others, then I had better be serious about it.

15

LEARNING TO TRUST

The ability to trust is lost as a result of child sexual abuse. Since I asked God to deliver me from the evil and violent assaults and they did not stop, I began to doubt that I could trust even God. I knew already that, as a child, there were many people in my life that I couldn't trust. At some point I stopped taking people and events at face value and looked intently for the evil behind any action or person. It made no difference if people were kind or harsh with me; I always expected something worse to come out of the interaction. From my perspective, everyone was guilty until proven innocent. My first assumption was that I could not trust a person, and I applied many tests before I allowed a person into my circle of trust. Very few ever joined that group. When one remains isolated and emotionally distant from others, trust is less of an issue. The relationship never becomes close enough that real trust is necessary. In most cases I remained emotionally distant keeping all at arms length.

A typical example was when I sensed that Liza and I were getting serious; I stood her up one weekend and made a spur of the moment weekend trip to my parent's farm in West Virginia. I took my roommate with me for the nearly 12-hour drive and left no word for Liza where I had gone or when I would see her again. I learned later that she had tried to locate me for several days and was quite worried. She began to believe that she had done something wrong to chase me away, when in fact we were simply becoming more comfortable with one another and that frightened me. I told her later that the trip to my parents was to tell them about her. My mother's concerns were that Liza came from a 'broken home' (her parents divorced when she was 13), she was a ballet dancer ("implying her character was questionable"), and she was a Baptist ("Why don't you find a good Catholic girl?"). My mother gave not a moment's thought to what kind of human being Liza was.

My experience in the support group challenged my historical pattern of distrust. I realized that everyone in the group was quickly well inside my circle of trust, but I had not put any of them through the performance tests to assure they were safe for me. This was a true leap of faith. Just as I had lost the ability to trust when my boundaries were repeatedly violated in so many destructive ways, I found that I began to regain the ability to trust by practicing it step-by-step with people in the support group. I believe we were practicing on each other. The first step of trust came on the first night when I opened up and told my story. My world did not crumble and I did not hear rumors, gossip, or criticisms as a result of what I had said. So I took another step. I repeated this cycle until most of the details of my story had been told. It took time for me to realize that I had related many of the most gruesome details of my abuse to this supportive group of folks, and it had all been received with compassion and understanding. In some ways it seemed that they had taken on part of my burden making it lighter for me.

The most important step of trust came between God and me. I had imputed to God all the evil of my priestly predators, and it took me time to understand the fallacy of this perspective. God did not cause or contribute to my abuse. However, He did give each person in my life a free will, which means each chose his or her own path. I accepted the reality that the evil was with the perpetrators and the violence was not a part of God's plan for me. This was validated as I became less bitter and more open to hearing and seeing how God was intervening in my life. It was also validated as I saw how the excruciating and violent evil of my youth was transformed into talents and skills that I could use each day to minister to others.

There were two very important facets to rebuilding my ability to trust. First was the reestablishment of meaningful and proper personal boundaries. I had progressed from a person with distorted boundaries to a person with boundaries so rigid, that trust and friendship were impossible. Neither extreme was where I wanted to be. My wife has over the years frequently told me that I function on a polar scale, bouncing from one extreme of emotion to the opposite extreme. Her frequent question of, "Tom, where is the middle ground with you?" never resulted in an explanation.

I had removed the thought and wisdom from the process of managing my personal boundaries, substituting a mechanical process based on the simple principle that no one could be trusted and each person had to earn even the most modest allotment of trust from me. As with my immediate family early on, even the slightest miscue pushed a person out of the circle of trust, rarely to be allowed back in. My new boundaries are biblically based, serious, and clearly defined.

The second facet for the rebuilding of my ability to trust was seeing the faith and character of the new people that God was placing in my life. While it started with the people of the support group, I found that the group grew rapidly as I worked more and more with VOICE. I think many of the people I met were looking for the same kind of safe and trustworthy people, and we helped each other relearn the discernment and skills of developing healthy relationships and true friendship.

16

WHO IS TOM SCALES TODAY?

I am very much a work in progress today. Without question, significant advances have been made. The life I live today is so different and so much more enjoyable and satisfying than the emotional isolation where I had simply survived before. Words cannot describe the feelings of freedom I have. The successes of the past serve as powerful motivators for me to continue healing and growing. It is a life-long journey. Discarding many of the self-destructive mind-sets and behaviors of the past has opened the door to new perspectives on healing and emboldened me to push forward to make them a reality in my life. I am thankful for each step and I take none of them for granted.

For years I hated the night and darkness. Both always felt dangerous for me because they were the venue where I relived my abuse over and over in my nightmares. But today they cause me no fear or trepidation and I find both to be sources of peace and calm.

I no longer work to hide. I work to shed light on the abuse I grew up with, so that others do not have to travel the same path. I work to provide an environment where survivors like me can break their silence and begin the healing process free of judgment and condemnation.

I no longer avoid people and I am certainly not shy about discussing my abuse and my path to healing. Having expelled guilt, shame and negative mental programming, I no longer need to be outside a group or cautiously measure each word or action I contribute.

I love life and the work I am doing. God has blessed me in ways I never thought possible. When I look over my shoulder today, I don't feel evil lurking, but I sense another of God's wonderful miracles coming my way. I no longer fear the future.

I have taken all the energy spent hiding my secret life and applied it to my adopted mission of breaking the silence and the cycle of child sexual abuse. Rather than feeling the constant burden of my past, I feel energized to work toward achieving the goals of my new life mission.

I have learned to build friendships and to keep them healthy and vibrant. I believe that every relationship in my life is better because of the progress I have made so far in healing. I believe I am building a legacy that I will be proud to leave behind.

I have compassion for predators thinking more about their path to destruction, rather than their current situation. What evil visited them? I look for ways that VOICE can intervene in their lives so that healing and restoration are possible?

In spite of all my progress, I know that more healing lies ahead and greater joy and peace are possible. Some day I expect to break down in a wash of tears and have the last vestiges of sadness, pain, and suffering excised from my heart and spirit as I continue on the road to become whole again. One cannot just create feelings and be cured. For them to surface in a real and meaningful way, the many self-protective walls and masks must be broken down and discarded forever. I am still discovering walls and masks hidden inside me. Just as some triggers have historically taken me back to the anguish of my childhood, it is my hope that there will be final cathartic triggers that will, once and for all, help me shatter the barriers that limit the fullness of my life.

As a survivor working to heal and have victory, one can sometimes sense and feel a whole different person inside. This persona is made up of a combination of dreams, desires, and an intuitive sense of the person that is possible. From these images springs a fountain of hope and positive anticipation. It is moments like these that tell me that a new life is not just possible but within my very grasp.

17

A FEW WORDS FOR SURVIVORS

I used to keep a piece of paper folded in my wallet that said: "Progress involves risk. You can't steal second base and keep your foot on first." From time to time I would take it out and read it as a reminder that progress requires courage, progress requires a willingness at times to challenge the status quo, and progress requires that you use your comfort zone as a launching point, not a crutch. Healing from child sexual abuse is much the same. You will meet people you trust and they will betray you. You will meet people who will tell you to "forget about it and move on," but that doesn't lead to healing. You will have family who will deny it ever happened and even ostracize you. You will be accused of destroying the family or a loved one. In many cases, the voices that deliver these messages to you hide their own shame and guilt or their inability to face the horrific nature of the violation. If they knew about the abuse and did nothing, admitting it happened, and worse – that it had a seriously damaging impact on you, places a burden on them that can be too heavy to carry. Denial is an easier path. Maybe they have to admit that Uncle Edgar or Aunt Suzie is a predator and they cannot face the conflict and family disruption that disclosing the truth will cause. Child sexual abuse is a crime but many lack the courage to support justice for the victim, rather they protect the abuser. They make the incredibly heartless choice to stick by their parents or spouses, rather than protect and support you. All of these responses and behaviors are designed to influence you to stay silent and accept your suffering for the good of the family or the family's reputation.

The persistence of these folks can wear you down or cause you to question your goal or motives – even your sanity. But it is important to always remember that you are precious in God's eyes. He does not want you to carry this burden for a lifetime. He wants you to reach out to Him, the ultimate healer of all, and cast your fears and burdens on Him. He will give you peace. He will give you the words and the courage to handle all of this in a Christ-like way. You do not need to be a Bible scholar, but searching the scriptures for wisdom, guidance, and comfort provides help without judgment or condemnation. Inner peace comes through prayer. Find courage through wisdom, and find support through safe and healthy relationships. If a relationship is not healthy, even if that person is your mother, father, sister, brother, neighbor, grandma or grandpa, keep them at a safe distance. That may even mean walking away from the relationship until you have the strength and healthy boundaries to handle it safely. God will provide you with the discernment to see the true character of people who want to be around you, or that you want to have around you. He will be your guide to making sound and positive choices about friendships.

As I stated earlier, my early life was XXX-rated and maybe yours was also. To protect myself, and in an effort to find some measure of happiness and self-esteem, I created many masks and compensating behaviors. What were yours? Did they include alcohol, eating disorders, cutting, lying, masturbation, and pornography, living in a fantasy world, isolation or abuse of others? You must believe that it does not have to stay that way. Healing is possible. Restoration is possible. Having and achieving dreams and a fulfilling life, is also possible. The most difficult step is frequently the first one, and make no mistake about it, healing and restoration are hard work. But the changed life is well worth the effort.

There is never a right time to break your silence. There is only today. You can start the healing process today, right now. Find a professional counselor, a trusted friend, or maybe a pastor, and begin the process of opening up about the abuse, reopening the wounds for hopefully the last time so that they can heal fully and finally. Feel free to contact VOICE Today at www.voicetoday.org. Reach out for joy, peace, happiness and true friendships. Never give up on that quest.

Amazing grace how sweet the sound
That saved a wretch like me!
I once was lost, but now am found,
Was blind, but now I see.